HEROES AND SPIES OF ZICHRON:

An Untold Story Behind
Building the Nation of Israel

By Vicki Jo Anderson

Heroes and Spies of Zichron:
An Untold Story Behind Building the Nation of Israel

Published by
Classic Ed Consulting
1670 Franquero Lane
Cottonwood, Az 86326

Printed in United States of America
ISBN: 978-0692843635

Acknowledgement of their kind support
and assistance: Steve Anderson, Doug and Jaydene Buhler,
Judy Naegle, Marsha Stratton, Jeanine Brown, Risa Bates

Other Books by this Author

The Other Eminent Men of Wilford Woodruff

History Reborn

This book is dedicated to one of the most effective, unpaid ambassadors Israel ever produced.

Dedicated to Dorit Dekel Hackett

ENDORSEMENTS

"I read with great interest the manuscript of *Heroes and Spies of Zichron: An Untold Story Behind Building the Nation of Israel.* I was genuinely touched by Sarah and the Aaronsohn's story. The Author tells the story in such an emotional, personal style, unique to herself. It is truly heartwarming. So many have previously addressed the topic of WWI Jewish Spies, the brutality of the Turks, the role of the British in the establishment of a Jewish nation, the Six Day War, and other related events. Most of these treatments are scientific, media-analyzed, mainstream, presentations. In this remarkable treatment, the Author personalizes these events as experienced by some of their most dedicated participants. The Jewish and Aaronsohn family legacies and oral histories, are unique, and personally, very touching. This book is a serious contribution to our understanding of some of the personal sacrifices made for Jewish freedom, and the possible intervention by Diety. This is a remarkable book! It is a non-fictional, personal, historical, narrative, that certainly deserves reading and pondering."

Clifford J. Stratton Ph.D.
Chief of Neuroscience, Emeritus.
University of Nevada, School of Medicine.
Genealogical Researcher and Author.

"It is an inspiring, gut-wrenching read. The format/framework is brilliant, like a story within a story. The present intertwined with the past. It would be a fabulous movie. It is as if you are taking the same walk with the Author. This book will assuredly inspire courage for those who perhaps may have a moral choice to make. None of us know the future, but the past can prepare us by example, such as these."

Judy Naegle
Author Classic Liberal Arts Instructor

An Amazing story! An Inspiring story! If Vicki Jo Anderson's *Hero's and Spies* wasn't documented history, you would believe it was a spy novel out of the mind of Brad Thor or Tom Clancy. Yet it's all true. Using first person accounts of the building of the nation-state of Israel, we come to learn the true cost of liberty and the price the righteous are willing to pay for it. Spy rings, cryptic coding, carrier pigeons, death-defying undercover operations; these are just a few of the tools and methods utilized by a small but God-fearing and dedicated band of Jewish Zionists in search of their promised land. Spanning a time period from pre-World War I through post-WWII, Anderson takes us on a journey as we follow righteous bands of freedom fighters through blood, sweat and tears, through wars great and small, and through inexplicable miracles from Heaven, all of which result in the establishment of the Jewish state of Israel. If you are a reader who wants to believe in the underdog who fights the good fight against all odds and comes out the victor, Anderson's *Hero's and Spies* is the page-turning, nail-biting, *must read* you've been looking for.

> Tim Ballard
> Author: *The Washington Hypothesis* and *The Lincoln Hypothesis*

TABLE OF CONTENTS

PREFACE

This combination of stories, as the reader will observe, crosses many years beginning around the 1880's to the present time. The conversations with Asher Dekel, for the sake of continuity, takes place over a period of two days, however there were many conversations this author had with Asher Dekel that took place over a number of years. Asher was Israeli. His daughter, who had married an American, was living in the United States when the three of us became acquainted. Over the course of a number of years we became fast friends. Each time I met with Asher, I had the great opportunity of asking him questions about the history of Israel and his own personal involvement in it. These stories have been put into a two-day event in this book to lend to the flow of history for the reader's sake. I actually did spend two different days in Israel with Asher and his lovely wife Sarah, but not consecutively as is written here. Most of the stories told in this history were communicated by Asher and augmented by further research to document the accuracy of each account.

It seemed like one story could not be told without leading into another as the whole history of modern Israel unfolded. The people involved are ordinary people, just like you and me. Never in their wildest imaginings would they have considered the possibility that they might do something that would impact history; and yet they did, all because they were true to what they felt they must do. They each acted in accordance with their deeply held convictions.

As you read the story of these ordinary folks, you will be able to see and feel that history turns on very small hinges; and perhaps in some nearly imperceptible way, you will be able to feel and know that we also are a part of history and your tiny part might just be what the world will need at this time.

The Author

FORWARD

Like author Vicki Jo Anderson I enjoy history, research, and reading. Vicki Jo and I grew up together in a small rural area of Northern Arizona, but each of us took very separate paths as adults. My career was that of a U.S. Naval Intelligence Officer followed by a Special Agent with the Naval Criminal Investigative Service (NCIS). With these careers I lived and worked throughout the world. I was introduced to, and worked with, peoples from a variety of religions and cultures. Perhaps it is this career that focused my attention on reading books of *history, biographies, political topics* and the like. Which leads me to this book.

When I began to read a draft manuscript of this book I could not put it down! This story contains all of the elements that I *crave* from a book. Additionally, it reads easily and smoothly. The storyline is wrapped within Vicki Jo's friendship with another woman, Dorit, who was born and raised in Israel but came to live for some years as an adult in Arizona.

I knew Dorit from her time in Arizona. She liked to share stories of her homeland and remembrances of her life there. Dorit was proud that she had served in the Israel Defense Forces, and she and I discussed and compared military life and the role of being a woman in such an environment.

What follows is the story of accidental friendship blossoming into familial feelings between Vicki Jo and Dorit; even though they differ in religion and upbringing, a lifelong bond is formed. Through Dorit, Vicki Jo is invited into the world of the formation of the nation of Israel. Vicki Jo understands there is a story that must be written, and so she does the research to uncover the facts, emotions and landscape of the story.

This book is an important read. Readers will *learn* from this book and they will be *inspired* by those whose stories it contains. This book showcases many core values instilled by families through generations, and invites the readers to contemplate their own values relating to family, religion and country.

Tricia Hance
Former NCIS Special Agent

ONE

HOW IT ALL BEGAN

Hebrew and Jewish Culture have always held a fascination for me. Some twenty years ago I heard about a Hebrew class being offered at a local Christian Church. My motivation to learn Hebrew was enhanced by my desire to be able to better understand the Old Testament and the culture and times in which they were written. Little did I know this interest would lead me to learn about the NILI spy organization and some of its members.

Not wanting to go alone, I invited my good friend Leslie White to go with me. She loved learning as much as I did. We were surprised when we arrived at the church and found a large number of people who were also interested in learning Hebrew. There must have been over thirty people there, anxious and interested for the class to begin. The teacher was a rather short, spunky gal, with beautiful auburn hair. Everything about her declared her linage. Her thick accent revealed that she was not native born. To this day I do not know how that Christian church was able to get her to come teach Hebrew, which was very tinged with Judaism.

As the class settled down the teacher introduced herself as Dorit Hackett. "Hackett," I thought, "I know the Hackett's, Hackett's are my neighbors!" I quickly reviewed in my mind how was it possible that this Jewish Hebrew teacher had a last name of Hackett. I reasoned that she must have married one of the Hackett boys. It was about that time that the teacher said that she was married to Bruce Hackett who is indeed the oldest son of my neighbors. I wondered how a Jewish girl from Israel had come to be married to my neighbor and to live in our little town of Cottonwood, Arizona. She continued with her story.

Bruce and Dorit Hackett

Dorit related to us that after high school, in Israel, she got the travel bug and wanted to see the world. While traveling in Colorado she met Bruce and found him to be the man of her dreams. Since then they have lived part of their married life in the United States and part in Israel.

Each class we attended held my friend and I in rapt attention. It seemed like we could not get enough of what Dorit was sharing. By contrast, as the months went by, the general interest in the class began to wane as it is very difficult to learn a new language and the newness began to wear off. After about five months there were only three students left, myself, Leslie, and one other, our good friend Susan. Since not any one of us three, or our teacher, belonged to the church where we were holding our classes, we were invited to find another place to meet. My husband graciously allowed us to use his office as it had a conference table. There the three of us had the wonderful experience with this master teacher for two more years.

It was a privilege to study and be tutored by Dorit. Each class was filled with not only the Hebrew language, but Judaism, and Jewish history as well. She did so much to expand our knowledge of the Old Testament. I loved every minute of it. If ever there was an ambassador of the religion, the race of Judah and the country of Israel, it was Dorit. She had such vast knowledge of Jewish theology and history that often we spent the whole class time spellbound by her insights. After sometime, I began to wonder how she had become so knowledgeable. She would often expound as a Rabbi would expound, introducing us into Jewish mysticism and other wonderful subjects. One day I asked Dorit just how she came to be so knowledgeable about her race and her religion. The following is a brief synopsis of her story.

Dorit was born in Tel Aviv, Israel in 1951. After she finished high school she served in the IDF (Israeli Defense Force) for two years from 1969-1970. Yes, she did carry an Uzi machine gun and always kept one at home as well.

Sarah, Dorit and Asher Dekel

She wrote the following in her own words:

"Since I grew up in a Jewish state, we studied the Old Testament again and again, from Kindergarten 'til we were done with high school. We learned history and Jewish history. Also, growing up being the first free generation after the "Shoah," (Holocaust) I grew up listening to many survivors from the camps, and learning from them how important it is to have hope." "The way we studied in the "old days" was the same way we tried to teach at American Heritage Academy [1] —about the whole world, and about Israel. It was just the way of life, doing all the traditions, the holidays, the traveling everywhere in Israel and being proud of being Israelis."

---

[1] * Author's note: My husband and I at the time were operating American Heritage Academy, an Arizona charter school. As a result of our friendship, Dorit became a Hebrew and guitar teacher for the academy.

Dorit continued: "When my son, Alon, was 10 years old, he was attacked by some kids on the playground in Daniel Bright School. He was called, "dirty Israeli." That day I knew that I had to do something. So I started a Hebrew school, and kids with their parents came from all over the valley. It was wonderful. I knew enough to start teaching, as the years went by. I went to classes for Hebrew schoolteachers, many workshops in Phoenix and got my lay rabbi certification from the Jewish conservative movement.

I also studied with Rabbi Albert Plotkin—may he rest in peace. He is one of a kind!!! He was a great person, amazing, knowledgeable, loving and the most important person in my Jewish education."

TWO

THE UNFOLDING STORY

Dorit was so well qualified to teach us. I hope we were as deserving as students. Throughout the course, in order to broaden our understanding, Dorit would refer and share different outside sources with us. One day she loaned me a book, a historical fiction novel, "No Time for Tears" by Cynthia Freeman. I was immediately attracted to the title. It gives an overall picture of the Jews in different parts of Europe before WWII, beautifully weaving the facts of real families with a fictitious family. This novel was so enlightening to me as it gave me insight into the Jewish drive to return to Israel.

There was one non-fiction family in the book that became written on my heart, the family was the Aaronsohns who immigrated to Israel from Romania in the 1882. I became connected to them, their story spoke personally to me and I wanted to know more.

There have been a few times in historical stories that I have felt myself becoming connected to certain people of the past. I think sometimes that I am like a youth who becomes so absorbed in his internet game that it is hard to leave it alone; with history, it is the same for me. I feel like I literally enter the past and these people become my friends and then I have a great desire for others to know their story and their greatness as I know it.

The Aaronsohn's story was a true story. I felt myself being drawn as if to a dear friend. Their story seemed to grab me and not let me go, or I grabbed them and didn't let them go. Either way, their story stayed with me. I had actually been reading the novel in preparation for our upcoming trip to Israel. Dorit's parents invited my husband and I, and my friend Leslie and her husband, to celebrate Passover with them in Israel.

Passover with the Dekels, Asher and Sarah, was such a rewarding experience. They were so gracious and we were in awe of the whole evening. Asher, as was customary, led the evening's events, inviting us to join in at the appropriate time.

Passover 1990: (L-R) Vicki Jo Anderson, Sarah Dekel, Steve Anderson, Dennis White, Leslie White, Asher Deckel

It all reminded me of the quote that, "one cannot appreciate the future without an understanding of the past." Passover certainly takes one on this journey.

As we ate our Passover meal, I asked Asher and his wife if they had ever heard of the Aaronsohn family. To my great delight, both them responded that Sarah and Aaron Aaronson were national heroes of Israel. Not only were they national heroes, but they were so happy to tell me that their childhood home was in the village where the Aaronsohns lived and helped settle the village of Zichron, ("Zee -kron"). Zichron is known as the one of the oldest towns in the modern history of Israel.

The village of Zichron was founded in 1882 by a group of Romanian Jews, who had lost their Romanian citizenship and sought a home in Israel. They dreamed of living in the land of their forefathers. They desired to live off the land, so pooling their money together they were able to buy a substantial parcel of land from a wealthy Arab in the northern part of what was then called Palestine. There they began to carve out a living from the barren, rocky soil. Many of them were inexperienced farmers and many others died of malaria. At this time over 80% of the land was total desert.

Though the Aaronsohns were knowledgeable farmers and they worked hard, the land seemed to resist all their efforts. When things were at the most possible black moment, when they thought they were not going to survive, a miracle occurred. The Baron Edmond de Rothchild, known as the "Great Benefactor," came to the aid of these early settlers. By his investment of money and introducing new ways of promoting agriculture, the settlers were able to establish a sustainable existence in that dry, arid region. The village was given a name Baron Rothchild. The complete name of the village is Zichron Ya'aakov. Zichron, in Hebrew means, a "memorable record" and Ya'aakov is Hebrew for Jacob. Jacob was the Baron's son who had passed away. The village was named in memory of his son.

I inquired if the story I had read about the NILI spy organization was true. Both Asher and his wife, Sarah, assured me that it was indeed true. They had grown up knowing older people in the village who had known the Aaronsohns and were there in the village at the time of Sarah's torture by the Turks.

As we were staying in Israel for two weeks they encouraged us to be sure and visit the village of Zichron and tour the home of the Aaronsohns, now a national historical site. The next morning we drove to a mountainous area, about thirty miles south of Haifa and about fifty miles north of Tel Aviv. Arriving in the beautiful village, much to my disappointment, we discovered that the Aaronson home was closed for the day. We couldn't see anything because the compound, which not only contains their two homes and several other buildings as well, is surrounded by a high stucco wall. The best I could do was walk around the outside of the enclosure.

I walked around the outside wall and pondered over the events that had taken place there, I felt that this home and family had a special role in the establishment of Israel. These people not only contributed to the fulfillment of ancient prophecy, but also helped in opening the way for the return of the Jews to their homeland. This experience never left me and I often gave it much thought.

Upon returning home to Arizona from our memorable trip, I began doing quite a bit of research into the Aaronsohns and the

NILI Spy organization. In all of my research, I always kept coming back to Sarah, I was so deeply touched by her and her noble spirit.

THREE

―――――――――――――――――――――

MOSHÉ DEKEL

Fast forward twenty some years from that event, my husband and I, with his sister and her husband, booked a Mediterranean cruise. One cruise port was Israel. By now, Dorit and her husband had moved back to Israel. I immediately contacted Dorit to see if we could meet up. It was decided that while Steve, my husband, and others went on the tour of Jerusalem, Dorit and her family would pick me up at the dock and we would go to Zichron. You can only imagine my excitement of having another chance at going back to Israel, to Zichron, and to the Aaronson home.

The next morning I was picked up at the entrance of the port by Dorit, her brother, Ya'ron, and her father, Asher. Ya'ron was conscripted to drive for us all. I knew Asher was going to be with us so I brought a hand held recorder to record his fascinating story of as a child being smuggled into Israel, his working with the Jewish resistance movement, and his participation in breaking the siege of Jerusalem. At the time of this conversation, Asher was about ninety years old, but his memory was still sharp.

It was so great to be back together again with these dear friends. We chatted awhile about a number of things. But I was so anxious to start the recording and get as much information from Asher as I could. This was a moment of a dream come true. Even though Asher was quite fluent in English, it still took him sometime to form his thoughts and his memories. I had so many questions that each time I asked one it seemed to throw off his thought process. I soon learned to stop asking so many questions and just let Asher talk and reminisce.

Asher's story begins with his father Moshé Dekel. Moshé lived in Poland. Before WWII there were many Jews living in Poland. Moshé began to have a feeling that he needed to go to the homeland of his ancestors, to the Holy Land, which at that time was called Palestine. But traveling through different countries was very difficult for Jews as there were many restrictions on what they could and could not do. Somewhere around the turn of the century, in the early 1900's, Moshé began his first attempt to travel to the Holy Land. This he did traveling all alone. Even though this was almost forty years before Hitler and WWII, the Jews were treated by most in Europe as "persona non gratis."

Jews were not allowed the required papers to travel between countries. This first attempt resulted in Moshé being caught in Romania. Because he didn't have traveling papers he was thrown in jail. Moshé didn't know how Jews in the city found out he was being held a prisoner, but they did. One day, the owner of a leather factory, a Jew, came to the jail and said he would put Moshé to work in his factory if they let him out. He went to "work" for this Jew and in two weeks they had a complete set of papers so he could return safely to Poland.

Not content to remain in Poland, Moshé made a second attempt to travel to the land of his forefathers only to be stopped, this time in Bulgaria. Not only was he stopped but, the crossing guards beat him so badly, that he was left deaf in one ear. Once again he was forced on a train and sent back to Poland.

After his second attempt and return to Poland, Moshé met and married 16 year old, Zipporah, who soon became pregnant. Even though he had a wife, and now a child on the way, Moshé once again began talking about his desire to go to the Holy land or Palestine. Not even a wife or the approaching birth of their new child could change his mind. Moshé's passion to go to Israel concerned his father very much and he tried every which way he could to dissuade his son from going, even to the point of disinheriting him.

Moshé's was not going because of some high adventure, his soul was responding to a very ancient prophecy regarding the return of the Jews to Jerusalem and the time was now. As difficult as it was for Zipporah, she understood the drive her husband had to go to Palestine. Moshé waited eight days until the circumcision ceremony of his new baby was performed. Then he left them and was again on his way. Now, more than ever, he was determined to raise his family in the land of his forefathers. This time, not only must he get there, but he must find a way for his little family to join him in Palestine. Moshé left for the third time and this time he made it.

Moshé arrived in Eratz Israel, as the Jews then called the land, somewhere between the years 1922-1923. It was known to the world as Palestine. His first objective was to make contact with some of his mother's relatives who were already living there. His relatives soon helped him to be able to find work. Moshé lived on very little, saving whatever he earned, so he could bring his wife and child to be with him. However, getting a certificate of entrance from the British who were controlling Israel, was another matter. It was over a year before Moshé could obtain from the British a certificate granting Zipporah and Asher permission to join him in Israel. In the meantime, Moshé worked to establish a home for his family in the mountainous village of Zichron.

In 1924, the ship carrying Zipporah and one year old Asher anchored off shore not far from Zichron. The British, at the time, were rather antagonistic and would not let the passengers unload and often sent them away. So the ship anchored a number of miles north of Tel Aviv. They were anchored some distance out because it was quite a rocky place. The British had also given full control of the docks and the incoming ships, including the loading and unloading to the Arabs.

Arab workers were paid to row out to the ships to unload loved ones as their families stood anxiously on the shore in anticipation of a long awaited reunion. Because there was no dock the only means of getting off these ships was to toss large rope cargo nets over the side allowing people to climb down. The climb was often made with all their earthly belongings on their back. But for babies, such as Asher, this was not an option. The Babies were dropped over the sides of the steamer by the sailors, from the deck of the ship to waiting hands in rowboats below. This was a tense moment for everyone, for all were hoping that the rowboat would not be rocked one way or the other by the rolling waves of water. For Zipporah and baby Asher all went well.

Finally, Moshé was reunited with his young wife and baby. What a joyous reunion for this little family! They had been separated for so long with very limited communication. Asher had often wondered what would have become of them if his father, Moshé, had not followed the promptings to go to Israel? Would Asher even be alive to tell his story?

**Moshé's family about 1931: Zipporah,
Tsevia, Asher, Moshé**

FOUR

FAMILY IN POLAND

Asher and his family often wondered what had happened to their relatives and friends of his parents who had remained in the Jewish community in Poland. Years later, Asher's younger brother, Tsevi, visited Poland to see where his parents and grandparents had lived. What he learned, as a result of his visit, left him forever grateful to his father Moshé, for his determination to go to Israel. He stood on the ruins of what was one of the largest Jewish ghettos in all of Europe. It was the Warsaw ghetto. He was informed that when the Nazis burned the ghetto, with thousands of Jews still inside, they burned it building by building. The destruction of the ghetto left rubble in some places as high as fifteen feet deep. The last place burned was the ghetto's synagogue.

The Nazis created the ghetto by forcing all the Jews of Poland into a small section of the city of Warsaw. Once the Jews gathered in the ghetto, the Nazis forced the Jews to build a large block wall around the ghetto. It was ten feet high with rolled barbwire on top. Large gates were installed to keep the Jews from leaving. The Jews could look down from their apartment buildings into the streets below and see Nazis and the Polish citizens coming and going about their daily lives. In addition to the some two hundred thousand Jews already in the ghetto, the Nazis shipped in an additional one hundred and fifty thousand Jews from all over Europe as well.

Not long after the wall was built 250,000 of the inhabitants were taken to a nearby death camp. It did not take long for those in the ghetto to learn of these deaths. The remaining Jews decided to defend themselves the best they could. When the Nazis came for the remaining Jews, they met the German soldiers with Molotov cocktails and smuggled rifles. Most of this ghetto resistance group consisted of young teenage boys. In an amazing feat of skill and bravery, the remaining Warsaw Jews were able to hold out against the Nazi's for 28 days. It was then that the Nazi's began to torch the ghetto building by building. It is estimated that some fifty thousand bodies remained entombed under the rubble. These Jews had chosen to die with honor, rather than die dishonored.

Yes, Asher still had many family members in Poland during WWII most of them were executed by the Nazis.

**(Left to Right:) Miri Dekel, Asher,
Ronen Gafniel, Yaron Dekel, Sarah Dekel**

FIVE

ZICHRON

According to Asher, the village of Zichron was a wonderful place to grow up. It was a kibbutz of sorts with its farms, orchards and fish hatcheries. As we left the area where they came ashore from the ship, the road began to climb. The hill to our right began to be more rocky and craggy. As the ocean dropped away below us, the cliffs began to appear as we climbed higher. Being from the Mountains in the West of the United States, it was not much of a hill, but for Israel, it was quite a hill. Little did I know we were beginning to climb the famous Mount Carmel. Up until now, the road had been following the shores of the Mediterranean Sea. We soon arrived at the somewhat secluded mountain village of Zichron. My excitement to be in Zichron once again was only enhanced by the simple beauty of the village.

Zichron is a quaint village with narrow, cobble stone type streets. The homes and businesses that line the Main Street make you feel like you are in a time warp and that you have been transported back to the early 1920's. Everything is so clean and fresh, all the flowers were in full bloom, leafy trees shading the sidewalks. People were eating at the open air, side -walk cafes. All were enjoying the mountain air. I felt like I was in some artist village in Colorado or Arizona. It reminded me of an old mining town near my home, Jerome, Arizona. Jerome also takes you back a step in time and is an artist community as well. The village of Zichron is not on a main road and is unknown to most tourists. Part of the special atmosphere that permeates this little village is to know the history of the heroes that were born and are buried there.

Main Street of Zichron

As we traveled down the narrow main street, the wall around the Aaronsohn's home began to appear, it is a chalked rose colored, stucco wall. We turned at the corner and parked in the back. I was excited to see that it was open this time. Once inside the wall, we noticed several buildings, two of which were residences. We began our visit in what appeared to have been some sort of warehouse. It is now a museum. A short video is shown of the life of the Aaronsohn family, their friends, Avshalom Fienberg, Na'aman Belkind and Joseph Lishansky, among others. The two Aaronsohn siblings highlighted were Aaron and Sarah. These two now are famous heroes in Israel. Sarah is known in Israel as the "Joan of Arc" of Israel, for her work in helping to create a homeland for the Jews.

The grounds, pathways and patios were all lined with either trees or flowers. It all was so inviting, one could not help but feel what a wonderful place it would have been in which to grow up. The two homes reminded me of the homes one would see in pictures of the Australian outback. They were built to combat the heat as best as possible, which included large porches. Near the patio was a weather station where members of the family recorded daily weather information. As we entered the first home I was taken aback how everything looked as if the Aaronsohns had just stepped out to run errands in town and would be right back. We were informed that almost all of the items in the house had actually belonged to the Aaronsohn family. As we passed from room to room we marveled at the items in the home that reflected their refined, educated and cultured life. There were paintings and many books. There was the piano that Sarah loved to play. There was the room where Aaron loved to do his agriculture experiments.

It was about this time that Asher reminded me that although he did not personally know Sarah or Aaron Aaronsohn, as both of them had been killed just a few years before his family arrived in Zichron, their extended family still lived in Zichron. Not only did he know members of the extended family, but, the story of these two heroes was often repeated among the villagers. It was a story that was told over and over again.

So who were the Aaronsohns and why is their story so captivating? The Aaronsohns family originally emigrated from Romania to Israel in 1882. They settled just north of what was then designated as Palestine. They purchased land from a wealthy Arab, who was more than happy to sell his useless real estate. Asher pointed out that it was in keeping with the Torah for the Jews to purchase the land. For Jeremiah the prophet wrote. "Yes, fields will once again be bought and sold—deeds signed and sealed and witnessed"

At that time, this area was under the rule of the Ottoman-Turks. The land was barren, forsaken, some areas, near the ocean were swampy and mosquito infested, with few people living in the area at that time, including Arabs. This was due to the land's inability to sustain many inhabitants

The Aaronsohn Home (now a museum) in Zichron

The family at once set to the arduous task of developing the land. Efrayim Aaronsohn, the father of this family, was a gifted farmer, even this desolate land, slowly began to respond to his watchful care. The conditions were extreme. With later Jewish families, they worked as a commune and gradually they were able to reap the reward of their hard labor. Their hard work combined with Baron Rothchild's investments and support made the village and the surrounding land increasingly sustainable for the growing community.

The Aaronsohn Family in Zichron about 1915

(Top) Aaron Aaronsohn; *(Center Row)* Rivka, Alexander Aaronsohn,
Shmuel Aaronsohn, Chaim Avraham; *(Lower Row)*
Sarah Aaronsohn, Efraim Fishel Aaronsohn

The Aaronsohn family consisted of the father, Efrayim, the mother, Malkahn, and six children. The six children were: Aaron, Rivkah, Shemuel, Sarah, Alexander, Zavi. All were bright, intelligent, mostly self educated and hard workers. Aaron and Sarah were instrumental in the founding, organizing, and leading the NILI Spy Organization. Alexander assisted his two siblings in helping to carrying out much of the work. This secret spy organization operated for several years at great risk to not only themselves but some forty others who worked with them. It was in directing this spy organization that Sarah gave her life in an effort to not disclose the names of the other members of the organization so that they might have a chance to escape and to live.

Unlike Sarah, who was born in Zichron, Aaron, the oldest brother, was born in Romania and was just six years old when his family moved to Eratz Israel. He, like his father, loved the land and loved agriculture.

With the backing and support of Baron Rothchild, Aaron was able to study and receive a degree from the agriculture college at Grignon, France. He taught for a while at a school owned by the Baron, but left after running into difficulties with the Baron's bureaucracy. He then worked in Turkey for a short time before returning to Eratz Israel.

Aaron Aaronsohn

In 1906, Aaron discovered a wild wheat in Galilee, called Emmer Wheat. It was hardy and could thrive in the harsh land of Israel. This discovery led the way for a food staple to be grown in Israel. Emmer wheat became the means to help sustain the increasing number of immigrants who were coming to the land. In addition to this discovery and because of his many agricultural experiments, Aaron published many articles worldwide that gave him a noted reputation among some of the leading scientist of the day.

He was invited to the United States by the Department of Agriculture and with their help he established an experimental agriculture station at Athlit, not far from Zichron, on the shore of the Mediterranean. He continued his agricultural studies discovering new methods and techniques for farming in this unique area. It was his practice to hire Arabs, as well as Jews. This caused friction with a number of the other members in the Zionist community. Zionists were those who were working for a Jewish homeland.

Aaron was invited to visit the United States numerous times. He was offered the prestigious position of head of the Department of Agronomy and Botany at the University of California Berkley. This department was the world leader in agricultural sciences at the time. The offer was difficult to turn down. Aaron felt that his mission and his work in life was to build the land of Israel and make it sustainable for the return of his people.

Aaron's sister Sarah, was born in Zichron in 1890, she was considered to be a part of the 'first native-born' of the land of Israel. Formal education for Sarah lasted until she was 12. Education in the Aaronsohn family was a lifelong quest. Sarah was fluent in Hebrew, Yiddish, French, Turkish, and could communicate some in Arabic. She eventually taught herself English as well. Loving the outdoor life, Sarah became an excellent rider and marksman. Because of her drive for knowledge Sarah became Aaron's agricultural assistant and traveled with him throughout Palestine as he went about collecting, and cataloging plants and minerals.

In 1914, Sarah married a wealthy businessman from Bulgaria, named Chaim Abraham. The couple moved to Istanbul. Little is known about this marriage other than it didn't last long and Sarah returned alone back to Israel. On her return trip, Sarah witnessed the Turks genocide of the Armenians. She wrote of the horrors which she observed, describing seeing hundreds of bodies of men, women, children and even babies. In another scene she saw five thousand Armenians bound to a pyramid of thorns and set on fire.

Sarah Aaronsohn

Sarah was never the same after witnessing these atrocities; she grew increasingly concerned for the survival of her own people, as the Turks had already begun persecuting the Jews in Israel. Their cruelty seemed to know no bounds. Jewish residents who did not have proper papers to stay in Israel were being deported at an alarming rate.

Sarah and Chaim Avraham

The Jewish Sarah and Chaim Avraham population had decreased from about eighty five thousand down to approximately fifty thousand at this time. Zionists became increasingly alarmed that the possibility of a Jewish homeland was in great jeopardy.

SIX

THE NILI SPY ORGANIZATION

When Sarah arrived back in Zichron after her long trip from Turkey, she discovered that her brother Aaron and their friend Abshalom Fienberg were already hard at work creating a spy organization in response to the situation. It was called the NILI Spy Organization. The name came from I Samuel 15:29, "The Eternity of Israel will not deceive." Other translations of the verse are, "The Eternal One of Israel will not deceive," and/or, "The God of Israel will not lie." The acronym of this verse is NILI.

The group laid out four goals:

1. To assist the British in conquering Eratz Israel by gathering Information.

2. To support the Jewish Yishu (community) with Relief fund Money, at a time of a famine and illness

3. To draw to the world's attention what was happening in Eratz Israel

4. To fulfill the dream of the establishment of a Jewish State in Eratz Israel

They had decided that it was best to secretly side with the British against the Turks. Others felt it was best to remain loyal to the Turks. Aaron and Abshalom felt that by working with the British, they had their best chance of establishing a homeland for the Jews. Aaron and Abshalom quickly took Sarah into their confidences. Actually, actions such as these were not new for the Aaronsohn family as their parents had always been Zionist.

Much to the organization's advantage and purpose a locust plague, spread across Israel in 1915. As the leading agronomist, Aaron was asked by the Turkish Pasha (leader) to study the plague as it was affecting the food supply of his troops. Traveling as his assistant, Sarah and Aaron traversed much of the Israel gathering data on the locusts. But this also gave them cover to gather data on the military strength, the number of divisions, the number of tanks, the movement of the troops, and their locations, etc. They also made contacts with others who were willing to gather information.

Because of his international travels, Aaron was able to make contact with the British in Egypt. However, it took him months to convince the British that the NILIS were reliable partners. It wasn't until Aaron traveled to London and gained support there, that he was finally able to convince Field Marshal Edmund Allenby to trust them and the information they were providing.

This was all taking place at the height of World War I. The Ottoman Turks had become allies of Germany. The British military stationed in Egypt had been assigned to push the Turks out of what was generally then known as Palestine. Because of their cruel and oppressive ways of governing, the Turks were hated by the Arabs and the Jews alike. The movie, "Lawrence of Arabia," made famous the efforts of the British officer T.E. Lawrence and his work with the Arabs to drive the Turks out of the Arabian areas at the same time the Aaronson's and their Jewish friends are helping the British drive the Turks out from Eratz Israel. British Field Marshal Allenby, who was stationed in Egypt, oversaw both operations.

While Aaron was traveling, he was able to contact the American Congress of Jews and convince them of the desperate situation of many of the Jews in Israel, many were without funds and many were near starvation. The American Jews rallied to the support of their fellow comrades and with each contact the NILIS made with the British, large amounts of money were transferred to the hands of the Aaronsohns, The Aaronsohns then distributed these funds to those in need.

In the beginning messages were transferred to waiting British warships in small rowboats under the cover of night near the agricultural station of Atlit, north of Zichron. Sometimes their friend, Yosef Lishanky, would swim out to the British ships with the message, if a small rowboat became too obvious. Other times, they used signal lights with coded messages. Then in 1917 German submarines (allies of the Turks) began patrolling the waters interrupting the ability of the NILI and the Aaronson's to make contact with the British ships. Not to be deterred, the organization took to sending homing carrier pigeons with coded messages.

Aaron had stayed in Egypt working with British Intelligence. This left the day-to- day operations of running the farm, directing of the spy organization and the distribution of the relief money, to Sarah. Sarah also had to care for the pigeons, gathering and coding and decoding their messages. She also kept contact with some forty individuals now involved in supplying information. At one point she traveled to Egypt to visit Aaron. Both Aaron and the British tried to convince her to stay, as it was no longer safe for her to remain in Israel. But Sarah would hear none of it. The memories of atrocities that she had seen in Armenia still remained with her and she was determine to do all in her power to save her people, so she returned once again to Israel.

Not long after her return to Zichron from Egypt, one of the carrier pigeons landed on the roof of the home of the Turkish Governor. The Turks immediately set about decoding the message. In the meantime Sarah and Abshalom decided that it was expedient to try another course, that of traveling to the border of Egypt, through the Sinai. Abshalom spoke fluent Arabic, so dressed as Bedouins, Abshalom and Yosef Lishansky left for Egypt with the latest message. Before they left for the arduous journey, Sarah convinced Abshalom to fill his pocket with some dates for food.

Abshalom and Lishansky were part way through the desert when they were attacked by Bedouins. Abshalom was killed in the attack. Fortunately, Lishansky was able to get away and continued, eventually making his way across the Sinai and to the British headquarters. Later, after delivering the message Lishansky returned to Israel where he was eventually caught and hung by the Turks in the public square.

After considerable effort, the Turks were able to decode the message they have found on the pigeon. This gave them enough information to seek out and round- up members of the spy organization. As they tortured some of the members they learned the names of others. Word soon arrived to Sarah that the Turks had found out who they were. She sent word to as many as she could to escape while they had a chance. Sarah chose not to flee, but instead remained in her home; there she waited for the Turks to come. She knew that as the leader of the NILIS she would be one of the first people they would come after. It has been speculated just why Sarah did not flee. Some say that she could not leave her aged father and others believe it was because she wanted to draw the Turks to her, thus giving time for other members of the spy group to escape, or to draw off the Turks and give time for Abshalom and Lishansky to get that last important message to the British. Perhaps all of these reasons were part of her motivation. But personal safety certainly did not play into her decision.

I was so lost in this story that I almost didn't catch that is was Asher asking the questions about Sarah, recounting at this time what the older members of the village had said. Some believed that Sarah was waiting for the Turks at the gate. Others said that she was playing the piano when they came. No matter what she was doing, she knew torture awaited her. Some villagers reported that her torture began with her having to witness them beating her aged father brutally before her own eyes. There is no recorded answer to these questions.

Asher continued relating that the most chilling part of villagers memories was to hear them tell of Sarah's tortured screams. For four relentless days the villagers listened helplessly, knowing that there was nothing they could do. It is so much a part of the story of Zichron, it seems that this is a memory that haunts the village even today. In spite of all that agony Sarah never broke or divulged any information to the Turks

The Turks saw that they were getting nowhere with Sarah, therefore they decided to take her to their dreaded Damascus Prison known for its torture. It was a place where nobody came out alive. The Turks were convinced they could then force her to talk. By this time Sarah knew that she had endured as much as was humanly possible and she knew that it was only a matter of time before she would find death at their hands. The burden and the fate of Israel, as she believed it, rested in her ability to protect others and to buy as much time as possible for everyone to get away and for all messages to be delivered.

She was determined to not break or reveal any information. Sarah asked permission to go to the house and change her bloody clothing before they left for the prison. A guard went with her. Unbeknown to the guard, hidden in the hollow of a wall near the bathroom was a small pistol. Sarah, fearing that she could not hold out any longer used the small pistol in an attempt to end her life. However, it was not a clean shot and for the next three days Sarah suffered excruciating pain before she died. However, it was not before Lishansky was able to deliver the final message to the British in Egypt.

Fragments of a note, written by Sarah, was found in the home after her death and it reads:

> *"Believe me I no longer have the strength to suffer and it would be better for me to kill myself than to be tortured under their bloodied hands…if we do not remember, you should [illegible].*
> *As heroes we died and did not confess…I aspired for my people and for my people's well being, and if my people is base—so be it."*

Even though the NILIS were eliminated, the British by this time had received more than enough information regarding the location of the Turkish forts, the placement of artillery, and number of troops, troop movements, supplies and supply lines. This gave the British more than enough information to begin its campaign against the Turks in Israel/Palestine. The British campaign was called the Southern Palestine Offensive. It began in Beersheba and moved north. The British knowledge was so complete that the Turks could not outmaneuver them. Once the British started in Beersheba there was no stopping until they had driven the Turks completely out of the land. This victorious campaign brought an end to the 400 years rule of the Ottoman Turks.

What a historic moment this was for the Jews of the world! Not since the time of Cyrus, King of Babylon, who lived in 500 B.C had any government or head of state supported a homeland for the Jews. The Jews had finally achieved a homeland after 2000 years without a country.

It is interesting to note that Sarah Aaronson died on October 7, 1917 and just twenty-four days later the Balfour Declaration was signed by the British Foreign Secretary, declaring a homeland for the Jews and less than a month later the British controlled Israel with a view to a homeland for the Jews. All had not been in vain. The NILI Spy Organization had helped change the history of the world in just eight short months of full operation.

The Balfour Declaration was a letter, signed by the British Foreign Secretary, Arthur James Balfour, written partly in anticipation of the British being victorious. It read:

> *"His Majesty's government view with favour, the establishment in Palestine of a national home for the Jewish people, and will use their best endeavours to facilitate the achievement of this object, it being clearly understood that nothing shall be done which may prejudice the civil and religious rights of existing non-Jewish communities in Palestine, or the rights and political status enjoyed by Jews in any other country."*

The British began to govern Israel in December 1917. The Balfour Declaration was later incorporated into the treaties signed after WWI as part of a Mandate for Palestine assigned to the British.

These treaties were signed by all the major powers of the world at that time. When the mandate came to an end in 1947, the League of Nations established the country of Israel as a homeland for the Jews.

Following the death of Sarah and other key members of the organization, Aaron continued to work as a world ambassador for the establishment of a Jewish homeland. Chaim Weizmann, who was the President of the Zionist Organization, and later became the first President of Israel, assigned Aaron to represent the Jewish homeland at the WWI Paris Peace treaty convention.

As mentioned before, Aaron was often at odds with other Zionist Jews who were opposed to employing Arabs. He even clashed over this issue with David Ben Gurion, who was one of the primary founders of Israel and its first Prime Minister. Aaron felt the two nationalities should be able to work together. The following is part of one of the working documents that appears to have Aaron's influence in it. It was written in January of 1919. This document was signed by Chaim Weizmann, head of the Zionist movement, and Emir Faisal the leader of the Arab forces. The preamble of the document read as follows:

"Mindful of the racial kinship and ancient bonds existing between the Arabs and the Jewish people. And realizing that the surest means of working out the consummation of their national aspirations, is through the closest possible collaboration in the development of the Arab State and Palestine, and being desirous further of confirming good understanding which exists between them, have agreed upon the following articles:"

Sadly, it was just five months later on May 15, 1917, Aaron, while on a British military flight crossing the English Channel to London, died when the plane crashed. Some say there is a certain mystery about the plane's crash that has never been explained.

The United States' special envoy to the Paris Peace Conference of 1919, said of Aaron:

> *"The Jewish race had many brilliant leaders but when Aaron died, I believe that it lost the man who, before all others, could kindle the hearts and minds of other nations to achieve sympathy. And not Zion alone will suffer for his loss."*

In a lecture given in 1919 at the Royal Military Academy at Woolwich, the Chief of the British Military Intelligence, General George Macdonogh, is quoted as saying:

> *"You will no doubt remember the great campaign of Lord Allenby in Palestine and perhaps you are surprised at the daring of his actions. Someone who is looking from the sidelines, lacking knowledge about the situation, is likely to think that Allenby took unwarranted risks."*
>
> *"That is not true. For Allenby knew with certainty from his intelligence (in Palestine) of all the preparations and all the movements of his enemy. All the cards of his enemy were revealed to him, and so he could play his hand with complete confidence. Under these conditions, victory was certain before he began."*

Without using their name this intelligence officer was giving NILI Spy organization credit for the British WWI victory over Germany's ally the Ottoman Empire.

General Edmund Allenby   **General George Macdonogh**

SEVEN

THE REST OF THE STORY

The land of Israel was now in the hands of the British. Up to this time the Aaronsohns and the whole spy organization had often been sabotaged by their own Zionist leaders, who felt that the work of the NILIS endangered the lives of the "Yishu." "Yishu" in Hebrew means the general body of Jews in Israel. Because of their conflict with the early Jewish leadership, the great work done by the Aaronsohns and the NILI Spy Organization was not recognized or acknowledged by the state of Israel until 1967.

The story of the Aaronsohns is so profound that on this trip I wanted to be able to absorb all that was going to be presented at their home and the museum. I didn't want to just see and learn, I wanted to feel and absorb as well.

As I slowly made my way around the lovely grounds, there were so many things that spoke of the family's industry and innovation. The Aaronsohn home, was filled with lovely and comfortable items, items of beauty and art. As I neared the end of the tour in the second house, a guide showed us a variety of different things that I do not now recall. I do remember seeing a small hidden panel in the wall near the bathroom. It was in this hollow space the family had placed a small revolver for any emergency that might arise. This is where Sarah retrieved the gun that she used to end her terrible torture. We then passed the bathroom where she had her only moment alone for four days and nights. There I sensed her terrible agony.

I knew our time at the Aaronsohns' home was coming to an end. But I didn't want it to come to an end. I felt as if I had just walked through history with some of the "greats." To be conscious that I was standing where one of the great events in history had taken place, to acknowledge the part that these basically unsung heroes played in restoration of the Jews to their ancient homeland, to realize that in spite of the fact that they, a very small group of people, from a very small village, on a very small mountain, yet they did very great things. They just did it.

I told Dorit, Yaron and Asher that I didn't want my time to end just yet. They responded that we were far from being finished in this walk through history. They informed me that we were going to the cemetery where Sarah was buried. I mentally said goodbye to the Aaronsohn home as we got in the car and began, once again to drive down Main Street.

As we turned onto the Main Street, and Yaron drove a few blocks, I asked if I could take a few minutes and walk the cobbled stone street. He stopped the car and indulged me in my wish. Not much had changed since Aaron and Sarah had walked those same streets. Most of the shops were made out of Sandstone with very thick walls to ward off the intense heat. On the corner we were met with a delicious aroma of pita bread being baked in a wood heated brick oven. It was irresistible.

Succumbing to the aroma we each indulged in a most delicious Mediterranean pita pocket.

We climbed back in the car and headed towards the east end of the village. In just a few blocks the road jogged a little and we turned left onto a dirt drive. The drive took us into the rather large, walled, Zichron village cemetery. It was a beautiful place with large trees scattered throughout, a sea of crowded graves greets all visitors. As is Jewish custom, each grave was covered with large cement slabs. Headstones of all sorts were on every grave. Headstones are required in all Jewish cemeteries.

At the entrance of the cemetery, there was a stainless steel, narrow sink with several water faucets. Attached to the sink was a pitcher. I watched as Dorit, Asher and Yaron filled the pitcher with water then poured that same water three times over each hand, letting their hands dry in the air. They then turned and filled the pitcher once again this time inviting me to participate with them. There was something special in getting to participate in this ancient rite of reverence and to be the object of their service.

Walking in, they took me to the lower part of the cemetery. Dorit informed me that we were going to see the graves of her grandparents. As we neared the concrete slab that covered their graves, my friends were ever so reverent. I watched them in silence, I almost felt like an intruder. After a few moments each one of them bent over and picked up a small rock and gently placed on the first grave and doing the same for the second grave. I learned that the putting of the small rock on the grave was a sign of respect and that it also let the departed loved one know that we had been there to honor them.

I followed their example wanting to honor their grandparents as well. It was only then that it truly dawned on me who we were honoring. It was Moshé and Zipporah! These were Asher's parents who immigrated to Israel from Poland so many long years ago. It was Moshé who had sacrificed so much! It was Moshé, who driven by some inner force, made three attempts to get to Israel. It was Moshé and Zipporah who came to Israel before it was free and before the land was sustainable.

These and many more thoughts began to run through my mind. Why had I been blessed with this great privilege? How was it that my little life in Cottonwood, Arizona, not only connected once, but twice with the Aaronsohns, and more particularly with Sarah, but also with Asher and his parents, Moshé and Zipporah, all of these amazing people had once called their little village of Zichron, home.

After spending sometime in this part of the cemetery, we then hiked up the hill to the upper part of the cemetery passing graves of several of their friends and relatives of Asher as we went. Dorit pointed to a rather secluded part of the cemetery under a large shade tree and said, "There you will find Sarah's grave." I walked up and around a number of graves to the large shade tree and there in this very crowded cemetery was the grave of Sarah, the "Joan of Arc" of Israel. I thought it was strange that her grave was the only one with a fence on either side of it. Later, I found out that because of the manner of her death, her grave had to be separated from the other graves.

I immediately looked around to find a small rock to place on her grave to let her know that I had come to honor her, that I had come to pay my respects and to pay homage in memory of her valiant soul. But I could not find a small rock, anywhere, it was as if all the rocks had been picked clean. It was only later that I learned that the schools now bring children every year to pay respect to Sarah's grave. No wonder, there was not a rock to be found—they had all been used.

Finally, after some scouting around, I found a small rock. I like to think of these small rocks as "honor rocks." In my mind, as I placed my rock, I so wanted her to know that I had come to honor her, I tried to express my admiration for her great courage and determination, for being true to the mission she felt she had been given in life. As I reviewed in my mind what horrors she stood against and what future she stood for, I knew that she had also touched my life, that one person can make a difference and that her life had made a great difference in mine. I was not the same person I was before I had learned of her and her determination. Leaving the cemetery we once again poured water over our hands.

Dorit informed me that we had one more stop before we were through for the day. It was late in the afternoon. She informed me that we were going to Hadera. Hadera is the hometown of Abshalom Fienberg. Because of the busy afternoon traffic, it took us about an hour to get to Hadera. The town of Hadera is rather hilly and almost as quaint as Zichron. There in the center of town is the boyhood home of Abshalom. It is also a designated historical site for Israel. We parked the car and walked into a beautiful Limestone patio that connects to a large limestone thick walled home. Dorit, said that before we went in she wanted to show me something outside. We walked around a limestone path to the front of the home. The front yard overlooks two streets that come together. There in the front corner of the yard was a beautifully formed palm date tree.

Invited by Dorit, I began reading the large brass sign that told the history of this palm tree. In 1967, all the Arab nations gathered with Egypt to attack Israel, to drive them out or exterminate them. In an amazing and miraculous turn of events the Israelis drove out the Arabs. They not only pushed them back, but for the first time since 1947 they gained control of Jerusalem. Israel conquered the Sinai as well, driving the Egyptians back across the Suez Canal.

Abshalom Feinberg
Father of Peace

When the battle in the Sinai came to end, an elderly Bedouin came up to one of the IDF officers and said he wanted to show him where his friend was located. The IDF commander was a bit confused, but followed the old man who led this Jewish commander to a spot in desert the Bedouins called," Kabir Yehudi," (the Jew's grave) There at this desert spot stood a lone date palm tree. The Bedouin pointed at the tree and said there is your friend. As they dug down they discovered the remains of a body, which later proved to be the remains of Abshalom Fienberg. The Date Palm tree had grown out of the dates in his pocket and the tree had been sustained and nourished by Abshalom's decaying body.

After reading the story on the plaque, I looked again at the beautiful date palm and realized that it had come as a start from that very same Date Palm tree that had grown out of Abshalom's pocket. It had grown from the very dates that Sarah had insisted Abshalom take with him for his desert crossing. I am not good at symbolisms, but to me this is very symbolic that their work did not die with them, that it lives and brings forth new life to others. It took almost 50 years from the time of Abshalom's death for Israel to finally reward this patriot son with full military honors. His remains are in the national military cemetery on Mount Herzel in Jerusalem.

It also took fifty years for the leaders of the Jewish community to acknowledge the sacrifices the members of the NILI Spy Organization made for the establishment of Israel. It had been out of fear that the Turks would do to "Yishuv" what they had done to the Armenians if they aligned themselves with the NILI or the British. It was a tough time, with no easy answers. The Yishuv leaders even threatened the organization with dire consequences if they didn't cease their activities and disband. The NILIS virtually had to stand alone.

After touring Abshalom's boyhood home, we sat on the patio eating a snack from the little café that is in the house. Night had fallen by now, and the evening stars were out. It was an evening that I didn't want to end. Everything that I had experienced that day had been so drenched in history. As I chatted with my friends it began to dawn on me that these three in their own right were part of a great unfolding story in the history of the Jewish people.

We had come that morning along the scenic route along the Mediterranean, but in returning we took a freeway that went through the middle of Tel Aviv. What an amazing modern city. It was rush hour traffic time and was pretty much stop and go. We arrived at the port at Ashdod and agreed to meet again the next morning to travel up to Jerusalem.

EIGHT

BRITISH RULE AND A NEW NATION

I was up bright and early the next morning, eager to meet my friends once again at the gate. I was so looking forward to another day of walking down history's engaging lane with Asher and his stories. When I got in the car, I once again turned on my recorder and started questioning Asher about his activities as a young man, trying to be cautious not to interrupt. Asher talked about the different roads we were traveling and told us how, as an operator of a bulldozer, he had helped to build some of those roads. Later, with a loan from his father, he was able to purchase his own bulldozer. After that he worked most of his married life for the post office.

He then began to reminisce about his youth when the British were in control of the land. All began well, but after a time, the British support for the Jews began to wane. Once again there were those in Yisuh that wanted to stand by the British no matter what and they tried to be good friends with the British. Others opposed the British and the things they were doing to support the Arab population, but not the Jewish population. The group who opposed

British rule also pushed for a Jewish state. Asher was allied with the first group, working with the British and wanting to help them.

One night, however, he was at a dance and the British soldiers came in and took two of his friends and they never saw or heard of them again. This changed Asher's allegiance and he began to give his full support to the group that opposed the British. This led to his joining the Jewish resistance movement. These two movements led to the Jews actually fighting among themselves.

Asher with Friends

The British fueled the resistance movement by doing such things as setting very low quotas for Jewish immigration, but allowing open immigration for Arabs. They allowed the Arab population to obtain and carry weapons while the Jews were barred from possessing any forms of arms. The British often made unannounced weapon searches in the Jewish homes and neighborhoods.

Asher and others in the resistance began their work with sticks or any other implements they could find. Asher recalls one night he and his buddies were able to get a British soldier so drunk that he passed out and that is how Asher obtained his first rifle. One of his assignments in the resistance was to hang flyers on walls around the city. This he did at night, because all British soldiers had orders to shoot on site anyone posting flyers. He was rather hesitant to talk too much about this period in his life and only shared a few sketchy details about his work in the resistance movement.

By 1939, officials in the British government in London were backtracking on the Balfour Declaration. A document called the White Paper, written in 1939, promoted the idea that with 240,000 Jews then in Israel, the intent of the Balfour Declaration, that declared Israel as a "homeland" for the Jews, had essentially been met. British leadership had changed and so did its attitude towards Israel. The British were operating under the treaty signed at the end of WW I and renewed by the League of Nation in 1923. These documents classified Palestine as a British Mandate.

In November of 1947 the United Nations created a resolution that effectively ended the British Mandate and rule of Palestine/Israel. The British intended to end their control of the land no matter how the U.N. General Assembly voted. Britain for sometime had been removing itself from most of their foreign colonies or rule. The resolution called for the creation of an independent Arab state and an independent Jewish state.

Palestine was essentially to be divided into two states, Arab Palestine and Jewish Israel.

It was a great celebration for the Jews when the United Nations, in 1947, passed the Partition ruling. A Jewish journalist, J. Zei Lurie, wrote of this miraculous vote:

> *"I remember the headline which I plastered in big bold type across the front page of the Hadasshah Newsletter, which I was editing on a part-time basis: U.N. DECLARES A JEWISH STATE."*
>
> *"A sovereign Jewish State, the first in 2,000 years. The joy in the tiny Jewish community of over half a million in Palestine, known as the Yisuv, was boundless. They were glued to their radios as the votes were counted on Nov. 29 (1947) Because of the seven-hour time difference, it was way after midnight when the majority was announced. They poured into the streets, shouting, dancing and drinking L'chaim to life."*

Israel was essentially created in a day, November 29, 1947, just as the prophet Isaiah had prophesized:

> *"Has a nation ever been born in a single day? Has a country ever come forth in a mere moment? But by the time Jerusalem's birth pains begin, her children will be born." Isaiah 66:8 NIV*

Although the land was to be divided into two separate states, Jerusalem, the plum jewel of all of Palestine, was to remain under the control of the United Nations, divided into its different sections, mainly a Jewish section and an Arab section, with a few other minority groups who lived there. The U. N. Partition Plan was widely accepted by the general Jewish public, but was completely rejected by the Arab leaders. Despite the Arabs objection the resolution creating the new lands passed.

NINE

SIX DAY WAR/MIRACLES

At the conclusion of the convention, civil war in Palestine began almost immediately. The Arabs began to march on Jerusalem. Six Arab nations joined the Palestinian Arabs to take all of Jerusalem first and then set about to conquer the rest of the country. They set siege on the city of Jerusalem that lasted six months. Their intent was to starve out the Jews of Jerusalem so they could say when the Jews left the city that they had abdicated and had given up any all claims to Jerusalem.

Seven months after the United Nations resolution, on May 14, 1948, the British left the land of Israel for good. Out of necessity by 1947 the Israelis had formed their own resistance groups. It was in this movement that Asher became an active participant. Within a year, by 1948, this rag tag group had become a regular army defending their country. Asher was now a member of the Israeli army, which was now called the IDF, Israeli Defense Force. In the beginning he was stationed just south of Tel Aviv.

As the British began to withdraw from around Jerusalem, they allowed the northern Arabs to not only take over their fort, but left them all their arms and ammunition. It was all out war on Jerusalem. Surrounded by Arab communities and attacking armies, the Jewish residents of the old city not only had the work of defending themselves, but of facing starvation as well, as a siege had been laid.

A short time into the siege the Arabs were able to cut off all the water that supplied the Jewish section. The Jewish commander, outside the city, sent orders for the fighters in the city to give up their vantage high point. From this point they had been able to keep the Arabs from coming too close to their section which had allowed for food to be brought in. This disturbing order left the small Jewish community within the walls virtually under siege by the Arabs with no water or food. The Arabs, with the British taking no action to stop them, began to attempt to starve out the Jews so that they could claim Jerusalem as all theirs. The British were set to leave on May 15, 1948. Everyone knew that it would be all out war once the British left. The State of Israel was just five months old and was still trying to fully organize and train their army and air force.

One of Asher's acquaintances was Louis Lenart, who had been an American fighter pilot in WWII. He is credited with saving Tel Aviv during this war, which is still today, called by the Jews, the War of Independence. He was born in Hungary, his family were Jewish farmers, and the family moved to the United States when he was just ten years old. At age 17 he enlisted in the United States Marine Corps and fought in the famous battle at Okinawa and other Pacific fronts. After his discharge he discovered that fourteen of his Hungarian relatives had died in Auschwitz.

Determined to do his part for his people, Lenart moved to Israel early in 1948 and joined in a clandestine effort to smuggle any surplus planes and parts in an attempt to create an air force for the fledgling country. On May 29, the large Egyptian air force advanced within 16 miles of Tel Aviv. Lenart, with only four other fighter pilots and planes made of salvaged pieces led the attack on the Egyptian columns. His four planes were able to completely destroy the part of the Egyptian air force that was attacking Tel Aviv. He is known through out Israel today, as "The man who saved Tel Aviv" and his story is part of the curriculum for Israeli school children.

Meanwhile, Jerusalem was on the verge of starvation from the siege. Attempts were made to send convoys of food from Tel Aviv up to Jerusalem. The road becomes rather steep as it climbs between the hills. Arab villages are on both sides of the road as it nears the top. When the food convoys from Tel Aviv would reach this spot, canons would ring out killing most of the occupants. Within minutes all the trucks would be emptied of their supplies and taken to the Arab village and armed forces.

The next attempts were made by welding large steel plates around the trucks to protect them from artillery and small arms weapons fire. The soldier nicknamed these trucks "sandwiches" for they were smashed between the large steel plates.

Asher was called up from his post, where he had been stationed south of Tel Aviv. He and another soldier were chosen to drive one of the "sandwiches" up in the next convoy. Knowing that the previous convoy had not made it through and most of the lives had been lost did not deter Asher. People were starving. That was what mattered.

His buddy received the orders to drive the truck. Asher sat in the front seat with his weapon across his lap. As they neared the top, near the pass, the cannons once again rang out and part of their truck was destroyed. Only this time, according to Asher, as he looked up he saw that this time it was the British that had blasted their truck. After the initial shock, Asher turned to his driver to see how he had faired in the blast. The cab was filled with blood and mangled body parts, but his friend was alive. As he tried to reach over to him he realized that his friend's arm had been severed and mangled in the blast and parts of his body were filled with shrapnel.

Asher quickly worked to staunch the flow of blood, as his friend was incapable of doing anything for himself. Asher tried to keep him conscious by continually talking to him, but he seemed to roll in and out of consciousness, being only vaguely aware of what was going on. Asher soon became cognizant that they were still being fired upon, not this time by artillery, but now by rifles. This time the shots were coming from Arabs.

Dodging flying bullets as best he could, Asher worked feverishly to get his friend from under the tangled metal. He was finally able to wriggle the driver out from under the damaged steering wheel. Wedging his door open Asher slid along the side of the truck, pulling his friend behind him. He had just a few seconds to make a quick decision on what to do next. Eyeing a ravine about thirty yards away and taking note of the brush for cover, Asher lifted his friend on his back and began to crawl towards the ravine. Asher is not a very big man, in his shoes he probably stands at five feet, five inches tall and is very lithe. But he was very physically fit, always had been. He related how he crawled for a long time. Crawling and hiking with his friend on his back, Asher hiked all through the night to get himself and his friend to safety. The next morning they arrived in the kiibbutz of Hulda.

Once arriving in Hulda, Asher's exhaustion knew no bounds. He slept for two days and two nights. There was a lot of activity in and around Hulda for it was the staging ground for the convoys. Throughout the duration of the siege over 230 trucks had been involved in trying to get food and water to Jews in Jerusalem. Hundreds had been killed trying to help.

At this point in our drive up to Jerusalem, we were so engulfed in his story, that we hardly understood him when he asked Yaron to pull over to the side of the road and stop. After Yaron found a place to pull over, Asher invited all of us to get out as he wanted to show us something. He began saying that the road we were on was the same road that the convoys took in their efforts to get food to Jerusalem. Asher then pointed down the hillside in the canyon to an abandoned, rusted, mangled truck. It was a 1940's model with obvious welded steel panels on the sides. There we saw one of the "sandwiches" or what was left of a sandwich. Much of the front and the cab had been blown apart.

Asher stood there a moment as we all stood looking at the battered truck. Pointing at the truck Asher said with some emotion, "That truck in the canyon is my truck." His comment left us dumbfounded for a minute. Asher further explained that It has been left there as a memorial to the great effort of the Jews to save their fellow Jews in Jerusalem.

These memorials also are left as a way to reinforce the idea of "Never Again."

To remember is a tenet of Judaism. The word "remember" is user over one hundred and twenty-five times in the Old Testament. Of all the 230 trucks, the one that has been left a memorial was the very one in which Asher and his friend had suffered and almost died in. As one travels around Israel a number of these memorials can be seen. One of the most moving memorials, for me, besides Asher's truck, was a bombed out school bus where little children had been killed.

We all stood looking at the truck mentally reliving his story in our minds. I could visualize Asher after the initial shock of finding his buddy so bloodied and maimed and yet here we were standing some fifty years later as tourists not only looking at the historical artifact, but listening to the very participant as well. Finding my words again I asked Asher what became of his friend, who had lost his arm. He responded happily, "Oh, he had a good life. He went on to become a school teacher and taught for many years and is now retired."

**Steelplated supply truck near road
from Tel Aviv to Jerusalem**

Asher would be sad if I didn't let the reader know, he wanted very much for the reader to understand that he did not intend to paint all of the British soldiers with a dark brush. He specifically talked about one British tank officer that came to their aid with two tanks in his command and helped protect the one of the convoys. Asher wished that he could remember his name, but he could not, it had been too long ago.

Getting back in the car I asked, "What finally happened to the Jews in the old city?" Asher was so full of details that reading a book couldn't have been any better. He described how another road was hastily constructed up a rather steep ridge that provided a way, under extreme road conditions for food and water to reach those inside the city. All Jews felt the imperative need to hold their place in the old city so that their claim to the ancient city could not be denied. Even though food and water was smuggled in, it was so very minimal at best. At one point the Jews in the city were forced to eat a wild weed called Mallow in order to survive.

The Arabs could not take the section by military assaults, so they began a methodical demolition of the houses one by one. This continued until the Jews were left in such a confined space that they had to surrender or be completely annihilated. The two rabbis of the city were the first to come out with white truce flags. That day, Jerusalem fell to the complete control of the Palestinian Arabs, led by Jordanian troops. Jerusalem remained in Arab control from 1948 to 1967.

Bombed-out homes—Jewish Section of Jerusalem

It was devastating to lose Jerusalem. But the Jews were able to effectively hold with their rag tag army the other area given to them by the United Nations partition plan. The three resistance groups, the "Irgun," the "Lehi," and the "Haganah" had all come together and formed the IDF in the 1947 war. Israel suffered its heaviest loses in this war, over 6,000 were killed.

Arriving in Jerusalem, we parked the car and headed to the Jaffa gate entrance to the old city. It was exciting to go into the old city, now having more background and a little more modern history of the city from Asher. We passed the different sections of the city, they in much the same area as they were in 1948. Today, all the sections are respected and generally respected. I also marveled at the multitude of different religious cites in and around Jerusalem that are protected and respected by the Israeli government. As we walked towards the Jewish section I tried to imagine the determination and the plight of the Jews in 1947.

Having had the privilege of being in the old city of Jerusalem before, I was not as intrigued with the ancient history of that city as I had been before. It was the modern history tumbling from Asher's memory that now held my attention. His historical recounting did not go into much detail of the years between 1947 and 1968 other than to observe that Israel suffered from continual terrorist attacks. He noted that each time Israel retaliated for one of these attacks, the U.N. managed to condemn the Jews for their retaliation, but never condemned the terrorist who perpetuated the attacks. In spite of the living under constant threats and attacks, Israel grew in population and advanced as a world economic power. Much credit for Israel's amazing economic growth and success must be given to the Jews in the United States. They, with other Jews from around the world, raised over 700 million dollars in aid to support and build the fledgling new state. Much of the aid went to fund their many defensive military actions.

Curious as to how Jerusalem finally came under Israel's full control, I asked Asher how that came about. He responded with a question asking me if I had ever heard of the "Six Day War" that took place in 1967. He continued without waiting for my answer, he said it all started on that fateful date of June 5, 1967. It was as if that day was burned into his memory. That day all the surrounding Arab countries joined in what they thought was a surprise attack on Israel. It was an all out war by the Arab state to wipe the State of Israel off the map and to annihilate the Jewish people. Dorit remembered exactly where she was when the war broke out. She said she was a high school student, but that day she was at home with her mother when they heard the sirens and fled for the shelter.

As the reminiscing about this war began to unfold, you could feel the energy in the car changing, because they all had experienced the Six Day War. Asher, as calm as ever, quietly asked again, "Do you know what happened during that war?" I responded years before I had read a book about it called, Fantastic Victory, by Cleon Skousen.

I knew that Abdul Nasser, the president of Egypt, had gathered the Arab nations to go to war against Israel. I also knew that the other front line armies were Syria, Jordan and that all the surrounding Arab nations had provided soldiers. President Nasser of Egypt had been trying for some time to provoke Israel into starting the war, so that

Israel would be seen as the aggressors. Nasser did this by sending military intrusions into the Sinai and harassing Israel in multiple ways. He also made a public broadcast promising to drive the Jews into the sea. He did a variety of things to create trouble for this fledgling country. He had the UN troops removed from the Suez Canal that served as a buffer between Israel and Egypt. He not only closed the Suez Canal to Israeli shipping, but had the Straits of Tiran closed as well. This effectively cut Israel's ability to maintain their commerce with the west. These closures had seriously affected Israel's economy.

Even the United States backed away from its earlier commitments in which they had promised to support Israel. The United States went so far as to establish an arms embargo against the fledgling country. France joined in and imposed its own embargo on arms to Israel as well. All the while the countries of Kuwait, Algeria, Saudi Arabia, Iraq were sending arms and troops to strengthen the Arab positions. Russia became the major supplier of airplanes, tanks and arms to the Arab forces.

The war soon started with Israeli farmers being fired on by Syria from the Golan Heights. Israel was acutely aware that thousands of soldiers and military equipment were poised to attack her from all sides inside and out. Crack Jordanian troops who controlled Jerusalem had been routinely threatening near by neighborhoods. Instinctively, Israel knew she had to act and to act quickly in order to survive.

They knew they stood little chance of survival if they waited to be attacked, so they went on the offensive. Israel was able to muster some 75,000 men, 175 jet planes and 1,000 tanks. The combined Arab forces mustered 450,000 men, 900 jet planes and 5,000 tanks. It was truly a David and Goliath situation. Israel decided to strike preemptively in an effort to keep the Arabs off Israeli soil. Egypt was its biggest threat so Israel decided to deal with Egypt first. This much, I told Asher, I did know.

Patiently, Asher had listened to me tell what I knew about the Six Day War. When I had finished he looked me in the eye and with great earnestness he asked me a second question. "Do you know about the miracles that transpired during this war?" I admitted that I did not know much other than little Israel had defeated the larger surrounding Arab countries. Intent on communicating this information to me, Asher began once again to talk in his quiet voice with his halting English. He seemed to think as he talked. It was if he was reliving so much of it in his mind and was trying to pick out certain parts that would be important to pass on.

He explained how he had been called up to work in communications between the branches of the IDF. He noted that the rabbis of Israel had begun to prepare for mass casualties expecting as many as 10,000 deaths to complete annihilation. They began preparing city parks as mass cemeteries.

On that fateful day of June 5, 1967, the Israeli planes took off early in the morning for Egypt. They circled wide over the Mediterranean as to not be tracked across the Sinai. Within forty-five minutes from the time these planes left Israel, the Israeli pilots had destroyed eighteen Egyptian airfields and 400 Egyptian aircraft. Within twelve hours the entire Egyptian Air force had been wiped out. Jordan had seen the planes leave on their radar and sent a coded message to Egypt. However, Egyptians had changed their code the day before and didn't realize that they were receiving a warning. They were completely taken by surprise. Israel's air force also destroyed two thirds of the Syrian air force.

After Egypt, one of the greatest concerns for the military was the town of Shechem, also known as Nablus by the Arabs. Thousands of Arabs lived in this town. It sits in a hill section leaving Jerusalem. Anyone wanting to enter must use a road that passes through rather high hills on either side. The Jordanians set up their tanks and mortar fire in this pass so that it would be all but impossible to reach Shechem/Nablus. Israeli commanders knew it would be suicide to try to take this route. They fought part of the Syria troops to the north and then entered the city from the direction of Syria. They were astounded when they marched into the city. Entering the town, the Israeli soldiers were warmly greeted as if they were in a large parade. The streets were lined with people who were cheering and waving white handkerchiefs as to honor the conquering heroes.

The soldiers thought this was a strange turn of events, but were thrilled that the people were welcoming them. In response some of the Israeli soldiers took out their handkerchiefs and waved back. Both parties were mistaken. Because the Israelis had come in from the direction of Syria, the people of Shechem/Nablus thought they were Syrian troops! It was not until an Israeli officer tried to take a rifle away from a guard that they discovered their mistake. But by then it was too late—the city was under Israeli control.

There were many more miracles, like the two paratroopers who had only their pistols and rifles. They were in the middle hot sands of the Sinai and saw a tank coming towards them. The tank had a total of eighteen soldiers in or on the tank. The two paratroopers decided they had nothing to lose so they locked their rifles on the tank and not only captured the tank, but the also eighteen soldiers. When the commander of the tank was asked why he didn't shoot them, he said his hands had been paralyzed and he couldn't move.

Egyptian troops in the Sinai were also met with dust storms in addition to a superbly executed blitz by the Israeli tanks. Arab tank commanders reported seeing tanks where there were no tanks. The Egyptian retreat was so disorganized that eventually 15,000 Arab soldiers died in the Sinai in a very short time.

The Golan Heights and the old city of Jerusalem proved to be one of Israel's greatest challenges. Once again a Syrian officer reported seeing "angels" on the heights and he didn't dare continue. By the end of the six days, Israel had not only won the war, but had quadrupled its land size, it had captured two billion dollars worth of Russian military equipment as well as two train loads of poisonous gas. Asher concluded by saying, "We don't believe in miracles, we depend on them."

The fight for the old city took some ten hours. When the soldiers entered the temple mound, many were crying. The Jews were finally home in the city of David. As a people, they had suffered for thousands of years, their destruction and exile was truly over. The city of David was theirs, just as God had promised. The scattered now could be gathered for the first time in over 2000 years. These events were literally the fulfillment of prophecy by ancient prophets. Isaiah, a Jewish prophet, proclaimed in the 8th century B.C., "In that day the Lord will reach out his hand a second time to bring back the remnant of his people..." (New Living Translation)

In just six days, Israel completed the greatest military victory in the history of the world. Just as God created the earth in six days and rested on the seventh. I asked Asher how he accounted for such an amazing feat by little Israel. He responded as many Israelis do, "You have to believe it was the finger of G-d. He created the earth in six days and then rested, we just do the same." "West Point," he continued, "won't study the Six Day War. " "You know why," he asked? I shook my head no. "They say that they only study tactics and strategies, not miracles. "

TEN

AN ENDING WITH A BEGINNING

I t was only then that we realized that it had grown dark. Like the day before, we had lingered much too long enjoying each other's company. However, we were now under a sense of urgency this time for my cruise ship was leaving at 9:00 sharp. We had yet a long way to go and it was still rush hour traffic.

When we reached the center of Tel Aviv, we encountered a massive wreck on the freeway. We sat for some time before it was cleaned up. I began mentally trying to figure out how I would catch up with my cruise ship if we didn't make it. I also wondered how my husband would feel if I didn't show up, as I had no means of communicating my predicament with him.

We arrived at the port security gate at 9:00 sharp. Because it was late, my friends were not allowed to drive me in. So they dropped me off at the gate and I began to run as best I could because I was still a quarter to a half–a-mile from the ship. That was not the worst of it. I had to run between large cargo containers and several giant moving container cranes, dodging them as best I could, as I had to run in almost complete darkness. The last stretch was an open lighted space about the size of a football field. I heard the ship's whistle blow and saw the men at the gangplank preparing its for retrieval. I was quite out of breath by then, but I felt a surge of energy as I tried to make them notice me. It worked and they noticed me and waited for me to arrive.

Once aboard the cruise ship I was greeted by a relieved husband and in-laws as well. As the ship pulled away from the dock, I stood on the deck looking back at the land of Ertaz Israel and felt like I had just come back out of a time warp. An overwhelming feeling came over me and I felt a strong impression, that the stories of Sarah, Aaron and Asher must not be lost. Deep down I felt I was to do my part to make this become a reality. I didn't know how, but I made a commitment that night that I would some day write about what I had learned and had been told.

Upon returning to the United States, my life became hectic and my commitment to write their stories soon took a back seat to the pressing issues of the day. Always though, in the back of my mind I knew, I had to keep my promise to write their story. On November 26, 2014, after a long battle against prostate cancer, Asher Dekel passed away at the age of 92. I did not learn of his death for several months.

The next May, just six months after Asher's death, I found myself with some time on my hands. I found my mind being filled with ideas, thoughts and memories of my Israel experience. I felt to pull out my dusty file on the Aaronsohns and my hand held recorder and listen to Asher once again. When I went on the Internet, I seemed to be able to find exactly what I needed to complete certain information. This happened almost every time I needed something, it was always there when I needed the information. Troves of information just seemed to open up.

Part of my hesitation had been my lack of talent for writing. I had tried to write several times before, but I never got far and found it a rather tedious task. But this time it was different, things began to fall in place. I did not feel like I was writing alone. Asher and Sarah didn't seem very far away. I felt their help and I could not stop this time until the manuscript was completed. In some ways I didn't want the project to come to an end, because I knew that our time together would end as well.

I don't know how much Hebrew language I learned from Dorit. But I gained an amazing knowledge of history and had the privilege of becoming acquainted with some of the greats in the making of Israel as a homeland for the Jews. I would even classify them as some of the greats who have ever walked this earth.

Why was I so blessed to have this priceless journey? I imagine if Asher heard me ask this question, he would probably hold up his hand and point upward and say, "It's the finger of G-d."

The great historian Will Durant said of the Jews "No people in history fought so tenaciously for liberty as the Jews, nor any other people against such odds."

Moshé Dekel
Born: Poland
Died: Zichron, Israel

Zipporah Dekel (lovingly called Zippi)
Born: Poland
Died: Zichron, Israel

Asher Dekel
Born: July 15, 1922, Poland
Died: November 26, 2014 Tel Aviv, Israel

Dorit Dekel Hacket
Born: 1951, Tel Aviv, Israel
Died:

Aaron Aaronsohn
Born: 1876 Bacău, Romania
Died: May 15, 1919 England

Sarah Aaronsohn
Born: January 5, 1890 Zichron, Israel
Died: October 9, 1917 Zichron, Israel

About the Author

Vicki Jo Anderson, a passionate history teacher and published author, armed with a double masters in History, using original source information about a Jewish Resistance group, brings to life the founding of Israel and the Nili Spy organization, often from the perspective of those who lived through it. Anderson is the author of *History Reborn* and *The Other Eminent Men of Wilford Woodruff.* Co-Founder of an Arizona Charter school and an accomplished high school teacher, Anderson has also served as an adjunct faculty member at several colleges. She is past President of Arizona Charter School Association, and has been a board member for multiple non-profits. Currently, Anderson is serving as President of the Board for Yes The Arc, an Arizona non-profit association that serves mentally handicapped adults.

* 9 7 8 0 6 9 2 8 4 3 6 3 5 *